"*A Lovely Light*"

A Dramatization in Three Acts
of the Poems and Letters of
Edna St. Vincent Millay

by

Dorothy Stickney

SAMUEL FRENCH, INC.
45 WEST 25TH STREET   NEW YORK 10010
7623 SUNSET BOULEVARD HOLLYWOOD 90046
LONDON   TORONTO

Copyright ©, 1958, 1982, by Dorothy Stickney

ALL RIGHTS RESERVED

CAUTION: Professionals and amateurs are hereby warned that A LOVELY LIGHT is subject to a royalty. It is fully protected under the copyright laws of the United States of America, the British Commonwealth, including Canada, and all other countries of the Copyright Union. All rights, including professional, amateur, motion pictures, recitation, lecturing, public reading, radio broadcasting, television, and the rights of translation into foreign languages are strictly reserved. In its present form the play is dedicated to the reading public only.

A LOVELY LIGHT may be given stage presentation by amateurs upon payment of a royalty of Fifty Dollars for the first performance, and Thirty-five Dollars for each additional performance, payable one week before the date when the play is given, to Samuel French, Inc., at 45 West 25th Street, New York, N.Y. 10010, or at 7623 Sunset Boulevard, Hollywood, CA. 90046, or to Samuel French (Canada), Ltd. 80 Richmond Street East, Toronto, Ontario, Canada M5C 1P1.

Royalty of the required amount must be paid whether the play is presented for charity or gain and whether or not admission is charged.

Stock royalty quoted on application to Samuel French, Inc.

For all other rights than those stipulated above, apply to International Creative Management, Inc., 40 West 57th Street, New York, N.Y. 10019.

Particular emphasis is laid on the question of amateur or professional readings, permission and terms for which must be secured in writing from Samuel French, Inc.

Copying from this book in whole or in part is strictly forbidden by law, and the right of performance is not transferable.

Whenever the play is produced the following notice must appear on all programs, printing and advertising for the play: "Produced by special arrangement with Samuel French, Inc."

Due authorship credit must be given on all programs, printing and advertising for the play.

Anyone presenting the play shall not commit or authorize any act or omission by which the copyright of the play or the right to copyright same may be impaired.

No changes shall be made in the play for the purpose of your production unless authorized in writing.

The publication of this play does not imply that it is necessarily available for performance by amateurs or professionals. Amateurs and professionals considering a production are strongly advised in their own interests to apply to Samuel French, Inc., for consent before starting rehearsals, advertising, or booking a theatre or hall.

No part of this book may be reproduced, stored in a retrieval system, or transmitted in any form, by any means, including mechanical, electronic, photocopying, recording, or otherwise, without the prior written permission of the publisher.

ISBN 0 573 63020 8   Printed in U.S.A.

COLLECTED POEMS OF EDNA ST. VINCENT MILLAY:
Copyright ©, 1917, 1921, 1922, 1923, 1928, 1931, 1933, 1934,
1936, 1937, 1938, 1939, 1940, 1941, 1950
by Edna St. Vincent Millay.

Copyright ©, 1945, 1946, 1947, 1951, 1952, 1953, 1954, 1956
by Norma Millay Ellis.

AN ANCIENT GESTURE:
Copyright ©, 1949 by Curtis Publishing Company.

LETTERS OF EDNA ST. VINCENT MILLAY:
Copyright ©, 1952 by Norma Millay Ellis.
Copyright ©, 1952 by Allan Ross Macdougall.

RENASCENCE AND SONNETS VI—XIV—XV:
Copyright ©, 1917, 1921, 1949 by Edna St. Vincent Millay.

THE PAEGAN PRAYER:
Copyright ©, 1936 by Edna St. Vincent Millay.

HUDSON THEATRE
Herman Bernstein, Lessee

S. HUROK

presents

DOROTHY STICKNEY

in

A LOVELY LIGHT

Directed by
HOWARD LINDSAY

A Dramatization of the Poems and Letters of
EDNA ST. VINCENT MILLAY

by
DOROTHY STICKNEY

Through arrangement with
NORMA MILLAY

Setting and Lighting by
LEE WATSON

Miss Stickney's Gown Designed by
HELENE PONS

INTRODUCTION

THE SETTING *for "A Lovely Light" is a limbo for the moods and for the illusions of time and place that are created by lighting. The background and masking, therefore, should be black. Platforms and steps must be lightly padded and painted black or covered with black fabric.*

The desk should be a wooden writing table, roughly forty-two by twenty inches in size, and not modern in design. It is Miss Millay's writing desk; with it should be a straight wooden chair without arms or upholstery. The bench is small and plain, about three feet by ten inches. It is a garden bench, perhaps seventeen inches high, dark and unobtrusive in color. The only other furniture is a large wing chair, of any dark color but with arms that one could sit upon.

A general standard for lighting is overall illumination (footlights included) plus independent circuits for special acting areas at the desk, bench, and wing chair. A follow spot and the 'Dawn' special are very important. Another circuit for the special acting area at Center is desirable, as is the 'Sun' special. All circuits should be dimmer controlled, for they are faded up and down, singly and in combination, throughout the show.

A diagram and basic cue sheets, which will further explain the setting, are enclosed. A dressing room will also be needed, with the usual facilities including electric outlets for our portable mirror lights. During the performance I will want some-

> one, in addition to the lighting operators, to control the house curtain.
>
> Miss .... and I will arrive, etc., (confirmation of itinerary). If your crew can be available soon thereafter, we can adjust the set, focus lights, and determine readings in preparation for a technical rehearsal sometime prior to performance. Since this rehearsal cannot take place until the setting is completed, and because time is often very limited, it is urgent that the technical work be as nearly completed as possible before we arrive.
>
> Miscellaneous (comments and queries by Miss ...., suggestions regarding scheduling of press conferences, interviews, receptions, and rehearsals) whenever practicable it is desirable to keep Miss .... free until curtain time on the day of the performance.
>
> Should you anticipate a problem or find that I may in any way be helpful, please feel free to call me collect at ....
>
> > Very truly yours,
> >
> > Stage Manager for "A Lovely Light"

A LOVELY LIGHT

ACT I

"The world stands out on either side
No wider than the heart is wide"

(To chair)

One night late in Autumn, Edna St. Vincent Millay sat at her desk working. She was alone—entirely alone in this house that had been her home for the past twenty-five years. It was an isolated house high in the Berkshire hills. The year was 1950—the month was October, and the time was five-thirty in the morning. She had been working all night. When she looked up the first light of dawn must have been coming through her window.

She turned off the desk lamp. Then she remembered to scribble a note to a woman from a neighboring farm who was coming that day to do the laundry. It was a note to caution her about a faulty electric iron. "And, Lena, be careful not to burn your fingers when you shift it from one heat to another. It's five-thirty and I've been working all night. I'm going to bed."

(Stand)

She straightened the scattered pages, then she

picked up a small glass of wine from the desk and started upstairs. Halfway up she carefully set the glass down on a step, without spilling a drop, and then she curled up on the landing like a tired child going to sleep, the sheaf of manuscript still in her hand.

(*To desk*)

The woman who came in the morning must have found the note and gone on with her work. Perhaps she had occasionally looked in from the kitchen, probably even called, and getting no answer, had concluded that either Miss Millay was still asleep, or that she was working in her study upstairs. The house was quiet—but then it was always quiet this last year. No one knew until many hours later that Edna St. Vincent Millay had died.

(*Stage dark—pin spot on face*)

> When shall I be dead?
> When my flesh is withered,
> And above my head
> Yellow pollen gathered
> All the empty afternoon?
> When sweet lovers pause and wonder
> Who am I that lie thereunder
> Hidden from the moon?
>
> This is my personal death?—
> That my lungs be failing
> To inhale the breath
> Others are exhaling?
> This my subtile spirits end?—
> Ah, when the thawed winter splashes
> Over these chance dust and ashes,
> Weep not me, my friend!

ACT I   A LOVELY LIGHT   9

> Me, by no means dead
> In that hour, but surely
> When this book, unread
> Rots to earth obscurely,
> And no more to any breast,
> Close against the clamorous swelling
> Of the thing there is no telling,
> Are these pages pressed!
>
> Stranger, pause and look;
> From the dust of ages
> Lift this little book,
> Turn the tattered pages,
> Read me, do not let me die!
> Search the fading letters, finding
> Steadfast in the broken binding
> All that once was I!

(Lights full up—move to front of desk)

This is the story of a woman told in her own words —the words of her letters and of her poems.

She grew up on the coast of Maine in the lovely little town of Camden. It was shaded by elms and maples. It was fragrant with sea water and New England garden flowers—or with the smell of pine trees and clean snow. Back of it was Mount Magunticook and in front of it was Penobscot Bay.

Now it is not yet daylight on a summer morning when she is very young.

(Center stage)

> You awake in wonder, you awake at half past four,
> Wondering what wonder is in store.
> You reach for your clothes in the dark and pull them on.

You have no time even to wash your face,
You have to climb Magunticook.
You run through the sleeping town, you do not arouse
Even a dog, you are so young and so light on your feet.
What a way to live, what a way—
No breakfast, not even hungry—an apple though, in the pocket,
And the only people you meet are store windows.
The path up the mountain is stony and in places steep,
And here it is really dark—wonderful, wonderful, wonderful—
The smell of bark and rotten leaves and dew!
And nobody awake in all the world but you,
Who lie on a high cliff until your elbows ache
To see the sun come up over Penobscot Bay.

Mrs. Millay had brought up her children alone from the time they were small. They were Norma, Kathleen and Edna St. Vincent, who was usually called Vincent. She supported them by doing, among other things, practical nursing. When the work took her away from home, her three little girls kept house by themselves. Vincent wrote to her adored mother.

(*Sit at desk*)

Camden, Maine. Mother dear:—and on Saturday, of course, we had baked beans and I had awfully good luck with them. Pascall's grocery bill is enclosed. We got the dollar you sent all right and what do you think we did? We went to see a play, "The Man On the Box." I'm sure you'd have wanted us to if you'd been here. Well—perhaps we shouldn't have done it—but Kathleen said she would put off getting her corsets, much as she wants them, until you could send another dollar. We wanted to go so bad.—Love from us all—Vincent.

(Crossing to chair)

> The railroad track is miles away,
> And the day is loud with voices speaking,
> Yet there isn't a train goes by all day
> But I hear its whistle shrieking.
> All night there isn't a train goes by,
> Though the night is still for sleep and dreaming,
> But I see its cinders red on the sky,
> And hear its engine steaming.
> My heart is warm with the friends I make;
> And better friends I'll not be knowing,
> Yet there isn't a train I wouldn't take
> No matter where it's going.

(Sit in wing back chair)

February 1913—YWCA—New York City. Dearest Mother and Norma and Kathleen: I rested beautifully in my berth last night. I tipped the porter too, this morning—a dime. Just think, I traveled Pullman all the way! From my window here I can see everything—just buildings though—it's buildings everywhere. Washings drying on lines strung between the houses, way up in the air. Children on roller skates playing tag down on the sidewalks—and cars and taxis—and NOISE! Yes, in New York you can *see* the noise! I don't mind the noise a bit. I can sleep better for it. I'll write you whenever I have time but I guess I'm going to be awfully busy.—Just basketsfull of love—Vincent.

April 1913—New York City. Dearest Darlings: I just this minute got a check for twenty-five dollars for two little poems—"God's World"—the one that begins "Oh World! I cannot hold thee close enough"—and "Travel"—you know—"The railroad track is miles away" etc. TWENTY-FIVE DOLLARS! I'm going to endorse it and send it home—after I've looked at it a little while. And Mother, promise me, please, that with some of this you'll do something to make something easier for yourself.—Shoes, dear, or have your glasses fixed if they're not just right. It's endorsed all right, isn't it? Oh Mother and girls!—Love, Vincent.

June 1917—Vassar College. Dear Family: In a few days I shall write myself A.B. Everything is all right, my bills are paid—but I must tell you something unpleasant which has just occurred. Because I was absent-minded and stayed out of town *one night*, forgetting that I had already lost my privileges because I stayed in New York a couple of days to go to the opera, the faculty has taken away from me my part in Commencement. That doesn't mean exactly what it says because my part in Commencement will go on—all the things I wrote—the baccalaureate hymn, the words to the tree ceremonies and all our songs and the marching song, but it will go on without me. I can't stay here at all for Commencement—my diploma will be shipped to me—like a codfish. The class is exceedingly indignant and is busy sending in petitions signed by scores of names and letters from representative people and all that. I never knew I had so many friends. It'll do no good. But it's a splendid row. I don't pretend I don't feel badly. I do. I've wept gallons—all over everybody. Never mind any inappropriate commencement gift.—Love, Vincent.

June 6, 1917. Dear Norma: Tell Mother it's all right. The class made such a fuss that they let me come back and I graduated in my cap and gown along with the rest—and had a wonderful time. I'm here in New York looking for a job. I have to start right in working as soon as I can. Everything costs so much I'm scared to death—so I must sell some poems. Please write me my darling, darling, darling sister.—Vincent Millay, A.B.

> We were very tired, we were very merry—
> We had gone back and forth all night on the ferry.
> It was bare and bright, and smelled like a stable—
> But we looked into a fire, we leaned across a table,
> We lay on a hill-top underneath the moon;
> And the whistles kept blowing, and the dawn came soon.
>
> We were very tired, we were very merry—
> We had gone back and forth all night on the ferry.
> And you ate an apple, and I ate a pear,
> From a dozen of each we had bought somewhere;
> And the sky went wan, and the wind came cold,
> And the sun rose dripping, a bucketful of gold.
>
> We were very tired, we were very merry—
> We had gone back and forth all night on the ferry.
> We hailed, "Good morrow, mother!" to a shawl-covered head,
> And bought a morning paper, which neither of us read;
> And she wept, "God bless you!" for the apples and pears,
> And we gave her all our money but our subway fares.

(Take Center Stage)

> My candle burns at both ends,
> It will not last the night;

> But Ah, my foes, and Oh, my friends,
> It gives a lovely light!
>
> Safe upon the solid rock the ugly houses stand:
> Come and see my shining palace built upon the sand!

1918—Greenwich Village. Dear Poetry Magazine: Spring is here and I could be very happy except that I am broke. Would you mind paying me now instead of on publication for those so stunning verses of mine which you have? I am become very thin and have taken to smoking Virginia tobacco. Wistfully yours, Edna St. Vincent Millay P.S. I am awfully broke. Would you mind paying me a lot?

Darling: I wish you were here. I have so many things to tell you that I can't write because it takes so long. I met a member of the Metropolitan Opera Company this summer—an Italian tenor—a thin one—and now I can speak Italian. I think I shall send this special delivery because I have more stamps than I need.

(Stand)

> I shall forget you presently, my dear,
> So make the most of this, your little day,
> Your little month, your little half a year,
> Ere I forget, or die, or move away,
> And we are done forever; by and by
> I shall forget you, as I said, but now,
> If you entreat me with your loveliest lie
> I will protest you with my favourite vow.
> I would indeed that love were longer-lived,
> And oaths were not so brittle as they are,
> But so it is, and nature has contrived

To struggle on without a break thus far,—
Whether or not we find what we are seeking
Is idle, biologically speaking.

Sweet Old Arthur: When are you coming back to New York? You said January, but I'm afraid you've changed your mind—and I have so wished to see you. You must by all means send me your new sonnets. I'm eager to see them. Arthur—you should always write in sonnet form—letters even. Vincent. P.S. I am earning a creditable living writing short stories under the name of Nancy Boyd. My second book of poems, which I am anxious for you to see, will be published this fall.

(*My candle burns at both ends*)

Dear Hal: You have by this time, I think, the proof of my two books but I am not sure you have a copy of "Aria da Capo," so I send you one. It is an unconscionable bunch of stuff to be wishing on a man, but it's your obsequies—I hope you were not intoxicated when you wired. Good friend, write me sometimes. It would afford me no end of innocent girlish pleasure. Vincent.

I'd better explain the Hal and the Arthur to whom she writes. Hal was a nickname for Whitter Bynner; Arthur was Arthur Davidson Ficke. They had been friends ever since their years in college together. They were charming, sophisticated men, and they were recognized poets with published books at the time when she was still living in Camden, Maine. As it happened, they'd been together when they first read her poem "Renascence." She had written it when she was barely nineteen years old and had entered it in a poetry contest. Hoping—I suppose—that it might win one of the cash prizes that were being offered. It hadn't won any prize at all but it had been published in an anthology—and Hal and Arthur had agreed that it lighted up the whole book. So they found out who and where she was and sent her an enthusiastic wire of admiration. "Renascence" is a long poem. This is the way it ends:

> The world stands out on either side
> No wider than the heart is wide;
> Above the world is stretched the sky,
> No higher than the soul is high.
> The heart can push the sea and land
> Farther away on either hand;
> The soul can split the sky in two,
> And let the face of God shine through.
> But East and West will pinch the heart
> That can not keep them pushed apart;
> And he whose soul is flat—the sky
> Will cave in on him by and by.

Arthur Ficke and Vincent had become devoted friends through the letters they had written each other—long before they finally met in New York. He was married at this time—a few years later there was a divorce—but all during those legendary Greenwich Village days Arthur and Hal and Vincent had been gay companions.

Spring 1920—Greenwich Village. Hal dear: My heart is breaking with envy of you. The day you set sail for the Orient I am going down to Chinatown and get a job scrubbing chow mein off teakwood tables with Old Dutch Cleanser. Ah me! And if you take Arthur with you—there is only one thing left. I shall asphyxiate myself in Pell Street punk smoke.

(*To chair*)

Summer 1920. Arthur dear: Please don't think me negligent or rude. I am both, in effect, of course, but please don't think me either—my mind is full of pounding steam like a radiator, and I am sodden with melancholy. I shall send back your sonnets in a day or two. I had to keep them a long time or my judgment on them would have been worthless. It is a pity you are so far away. There are so few people in the world to whom one has a word to say, Arthur. Write me sometimes—I shall always care for what you are thinking. Vincent.

Dear Hal and Arthur: When are you two boys coming back here? Where you used to be there is a hole in the world, which I find myself constantly walking around in the daytime and falling into at night. I miss you like hell—but aside from that I am having a terribly nice time. Also, I am becoming very famous. The current Vanity Fair has a whole page of my poems, and a photograph of me that looks about as much like me as it does like Arnold Bennett. Besides, I just got a prize of a hundred dollars in Poetry Magazine for "Beanstalk". And I'm spending it all on clothes!

(*Rising from chair*)

> Ho, Giant! This is I!
> I have built me a bean-stalk into your sky!
> La—but it's lovely, up so high!
>
> This is how I came—I put
> Here my knee, there my foot,
> Up and up, from shoot to shoot—
> And the blessed bean-stalk thinning
> Like the mischief all the time,
> Till it took me rocking, spinning,

In a dizzy, sunny circle,
Making angles with the root,
Far and out above the cackle
Of the city I was born in,
Till the little dirty city
In the light so sheer and sunny
Shone as dazzling bright and pretty
As the money that you find
In a dream of finding money—
What a wind! What a morning!

P.S. The Poetry Society of America is raising its dues. I daresay many people are indignant, but as for me I take it all in a very equitable frame of mind. Big or little it's all the same to me since I don't pay them anyway. This is a very silly letter I've written. It is not at all what I wanted to say to you, my cherished friends. But perhaps you would as soon have me silly as sad, and I am sad so much of the time no matter what kind of letter I write. Goodnight, and forgive my chattering.—Vincent.

(*Seated in chair*)

Autumn—1920. Arthur: I love you too, my dear, and shall always, just as I did the first moment I saw you. Sometimes at night when you were in France during the war I would read over the sonnets you had sent me—just as you've been doing now with mine, and long for you. It seemed incredible that you were not in the same room with me, you were so much nearer than anything else, nearer than the dress I was wearing. It doesn't matter at all that we never see each other and that we write so seldom. We shall never escape from each other. It is very dear to me to know that you love me, Arthur, just as I love you, quietly, quietly, yet with all your strength, and with a strength greater than your own, that drives you toward me like a wind. It is a thing that exists simply, like a sapphire—like anything roundly beautiful. There is nothing to be done about it—and nothing one would wish to do. It is as if I knew of a swamp of violets and wanted to take you there and share them with you because you are my friend. But all that is the least of it, my dear. You will never grow old to me, or die, or be lost in any way. Vincent.

> Love in the open hand, no thing but that,
> Ungemmed, unhidden, wishing not to hurt,
> As one should bring you cowslips in a hat
> Swung from the hand, or apples in her skirt,
> I bring you, calling out as children do:
> "Look what I have!—And these are all for you"

(Walk to desk)

She had said, "There is nothing to be done about it, and nothing one would wish to do." She had also said, "It doesn't matter at all that we never see each other and that we write so seldom."—But it did matter. Gradually she began to realize that it did matter.

> Pity me not because the light of day
> At close of day no longer walks the sky;
> Pity me not for beauties passed away
> From field and thicket as the year goes by;
> Pity me not the waning of the moon,
> Nor that the ebbing tide goes out to sea,
> Nor that a man's desire is hushed so soon,
> And you no longer look with love on me.
> This have I known always; Love is no more
> Than the wide blossom which the wind assails,
> Than the great tide that treads the shifting shore,
> Strewing fresh wreckage gathered in the gales:

> Pity me that the heart is slow to learn
> What the swift mind beholds at every turn.

(*Sitting at desk*)

Winter 1920. Dearest beloved Mother: The reason I have not written you for so long is because I have been sick.—I'm all right again now, but I had bronchitis for a while, and after that another small nervous breakdown. I didn't want you to know for fear you would worry. I have decided that the thing for me to do is to have a change—a change of everything. So I'm going to Europe. My poetry needs fresh grass to feed on. Technically, I'm going as European Correspondent for Vanity Fair. I shall be perfectly happy and safe, because I speak French and because I am a very capable and sensible woman when I am left to myself.—You know that, dear. And Mother dear, this is the whole thing. Just as I've told it. It has nothing to do with any love affair past or present. Forgive me for not writing before. I've been sick, you see. Your devoted daughter.

(*While crossing to chair.*)

> Thanks be to God the world is wide
> And I am going far from home,
> For I forgot in Camelot
> The man I loved in Rome.
>
> And I forgot in Kensington
> The man I loved in Kew;
> And there must be a place for me
> To think no more of you.

September 1921—France. Dearest Norma: I know the greatest joke on the French people. They don't eat blackberries! They think they're poison! They eat every other damn thing you can imagine—frogs, mussels, periwinkels, snails, etc., but they are convinced that blackberries are poison and they never touch 'em. So as far as I can see, all the blackberries in Northern France are living and having their being and ripening in the sun for my personal delectation.

> Time does not bring relief; you all have lied
> Who told me time would ease me of my pain!
> I miss him in the weeping of the rain;
> I want him at the shrinking of the tide;
> The old snows melt from every mountain-side
> And last year's leaves are smoke in every lane;
> But last year's bitter loving must remain
> Heaped on my heart, and my old thoughts abide.
> There are a hundred places where I fear
> To go,—so with his memory they brim.
> And entering with relief some quiet place
> Where never fell his foot or shone his face
> I say, "There is no memory of him here!"
> And so stand stricken, so remembering him.

October 1921—Albania. Arthur my dearest: When I come back to the States, won't you come east to see me? I know you can't come to Europe but you could come to New York because you often do, to see Hal or somebody. Would it not be wonderful to be together again, for a little while? Arthur, it's wicked and useless all these months and months apart from you—all these years with only a glimpse of you in the face of everybody. Whatever happens, I want to see you again, Arthur?

(Stage black except for pin spot on face)

> Night is my sister, and how deep in love,

How drowned in love and weedily washed ashore,
There to be fretted by the drag and shove
At the tide's edge, I lie.—these things and more:
Whose arm alone between me and the sand,
Whose voice alone, whose pitiful breath brought
   near,
Could thaw these nostrils and unlock this hand,
She could advise you, should you care to hear.
Small chance, however, in a storm so black,
A man will leave his friendly fire and snug
For a drowned woman's sake, and bring her back
To drip and scatter shells upon the rug.
No one but Night with tears on her dark face,
Watches beside me in this windy place.

(*Lights up full*)

January 1922. Vienna. Arthur: My dear, I knew all about the girl in New York long before you told me. At least, of course I knew nothing at all about her but I knew what had happened. After the divorce I knew when you were to be in New York and while you were there I thought of you and I said to myself, "He's falling in love with some girl there." Then, you see, you didn't write me while you were there and after that your letters were different a little little bit, anyway, I knew. It doesn't matter. All that has nothing to do with what we are to each other—nothing at all to do with you and me. We know each other in such a terrible, certain, windless way. You and I have almost achieved that which is never achieved. We sit in each other's souls.

December 1922—France. Arthur dear: Isn't it funny about you and Gladys? My God it's marvelous! You don't need to tell me what a nice girl she is—nicer than that! I know in my way just as you know in your way how nice she is. Can't fool me. I knew it the minute I set eyes on her. And you didn't think we'd like each other. Huh! Men don't know very much. Is this a snippy letter, dear?—No it isn't. I shall love you till the day I die—though I shan't always be thinking about it, thank God! Yet, I shall be thinking about it every time I think about you, that's sure. With love, Vincent.

> Well, I have lost you; and I lost you fairly;
> In my own way, and with my full consent.
> Say what you will, kings in a tumbrel rarely
> Went to their deaths more proud than this one went.
> Some nights of apprehension and hot weeping
> I will confess; but that's permitted me;
> Day dried my eyes; I was not one for keeping
> Rubbed in a cage a wing that would be free.
> If I had loved you less or played you slyly
> I might have held you for a summer more,
> But at the cost of words I value highly,
> And no such summer as the one before.
> Should I outlive this anguish—and men do—
> I shall have only good to say of you.

CURTAIN

ACT II

"I know not how things can be!
I breathed my soul back into me."

People dress and go to town;
I sit in my chair.
All my thoughts are slow and brown:
Standing up or sitting down,
Little matters, or what gown
Or what shoes I wear.

(*Light full up*)

Shillingstone, Dorset, England. Dearest Norma: I'm writing this letter in my little whitewashed and straw carpeted hut in Dorset, up in a field under the Downs. I stay here by myself most all day and scarcely see a living soul except the animals. It's beautiful. You'd love it. Yes, I have been sick but I'm much better now—and I'm working terribly hard. Mother is wonderful. She went bouncing all over Europe with me. I'll never cease to be grateful that I was able to bring her abroad while she is, to all intents and purposes, young. I've been chewing some of the spruce gum that Kathleen sent Mother from Maine. I can just see the tree she dug it from. I know just how the bark looked.

My heart, being hungry, feeds on food
The fat of heart despise.

Beauty where beauty never stood,
And sweet where no sweet lies
I gather to my querulous need
Having a growing heart to feed.

It may be, when my heart is dull,
Having attained its girth,
I shall not find so beautiful
The meagre shapes of Earth.
Nor linger in the rain to mark
The smell of tansy through the dark.

Sweet old Arthur: I'm having a fine time. Gladys is here living just down the road from me, and has a horse to ride and looks handsome in her riding clothes. I have discovered that she paints damn well. Why didn't you tell me?

(*Walk to desk*)

Kathleen dear: I wish you would get out of the library some books about the Einstein Theory of Relativity. The whole thing is fascinating and I long for you to talk it over with. It stretches the mind. It's a wonderful cold bath for the imagination.—Love to you, Darling.

And all is over that could come to pass
Last year; excepting this: the mind is free
One moment, to compute, refute, amass,
Catalogue, question, contemplate, and see.

Dearest Norma: It is nearly two years since I sailed from Pier 57. Mother and I are rather looking forward to leaving England now. It has been so cold and disagreeable. Some day before very long, dear, I shall see you again.

They came back to America early in the spring. Mrs.

Millay returned to her home in Maine and Vincent stayed on in New York. She wrote to a friend—

(*Sitting at desk*)

May 2nd, New York.—and I know Frank Crownenshield is terribly peeved at me. He thinks, I'm sure, that the reason I've not been writing anything for Vanity Fair lately is because I'm writing for the Saturday Evening Post or something. Truth is, I've not put pen to paper for anybody—not even for myself—in months. Please tell Crowney not to be angry with me. I will write him too. And give my love to Elinore Wylie.

May 30, 1923. Dearest Mother: You must need money, dear. Let me know as soon as you get this and I will send you some. I haven't, at the moment, a great deal (except for my Pulitzer Prize of a thousand bucks) which I ain't going to bust for God or hero—but I'll send you a little and there will be more coming.

(*Rising from desk*)

Mother, I've been a bad girl not to write you but you'll forgive me when you know my excuse. Darling, do you remember meeting Eugen Boissevain one day in Waverly Place? It was only for a moment, so possibly you don't remember. But anyway, you will like him very much when you know him, which will be soon. AND it is important that you should like him, BECAUSE I love him very much and am going to marry him.—THERE.—We shall be married sometime this summer.

Eugen Boissevain was a well-to-do coffee importer from Holland. He had good looks, abundant vitality, and a fine boisterous laugh. He was a big man—kind and generous. He spoke with a slight accent, and was, in his own words, 'A typical Dutchman—half French and half Irish.'

(*Sitting in chair*)

Darling Mother: At last I'm doing what I should have done ages ago. Having an excellent diagnostician examine me thoroughly and 'board me out' to all kinds of specialists. I'm allowed to work only one hour a day now and must be pretty quiet and see almost nobody. Don't be the least bit alarmed dearest. I don't feel badly at all. I'm just being taken care of and helped to get perfectly well, you see. Eugen has been taking me to all these doctors. Probably by myself I would never have done it. You will like him, Mother. Love and love and love, Vincent.

They were married in July of 1923, and as Eugen Boissevain had previously arranged, on the afternoon of their wedding day Vincent entered a hospital for the operation which may have saved her life. It's a pity so few of their letters exist. Of course, few were ever written because for the next twenty-four years they were seldom apart from each other. One rare exception was during the first year of their marriage. A reading tour had already been contracted for and of course the obligation had to be met, so as soon as Vincent was strong enough—no, before she was strong enough, she started out.

I shall soon depart this life and leave for Pittsburgh and points west on a reading tour.

January 1924. Chicago & Northwestern Station. Darling Eugen: I have just made my train and here I sit.

Did you ever go from Chicago west in a so-called Parlor car? Well don't. In a day coach, if you're lucky you can get a seat by a window and look out; whereas, in a parlor car your chair is nailed with its back to the window so you couldn't possibly see a thing even if you should want to—which, I should say, is extremely unlikely. Everyone who looks at me wonders why such a nice girl with such a beautiful gold pencil and such expensive cufflinks and such a refined and elegant notebook has such dirty hands. I don't care. I'm tired of washing my hands. It's a great waste of time. Besides, in winter it's dangerous.

February 1924. Cedar Rapids, Iowa. All your letters came—even the ones that forgot to say 'Iowa.' It's curious I have been so—unable to write to you lately. I seem sunk in a lethargy too deep for action of any kind, and I haven't wanted you—oh darling, least of all you—to see how footsore and—dusty I am.

I got through my reading well enough yesterday. The one in the afternoon was a great success—crowded house, etc. BUT the one in the evening—the one in the evening was in a private house. A bunch of wealthy people came together to see what I looked like and to bet with each other how many of my naughty poems I'd dare to read. Oh Lord! If ever I felt like a prostitute it was last night. I just kept saying over and over to myself, 'Never mind, it's a hundred and fifty dollars.'

(*Pick up book from desk. Cross behind desk, take center stage and bow to imaginary audience.*)

This sonnet is called *Epitaph For The Race Of Man*.

> Read history: thus learn how small a space
> You may inhabit, nor inhabit long
> In crowding Cosmos—in that confined place

Work boldly; build your flimsy barriers strong;
Turn round and round, make warm your nest; among
The other hunting beasts, keep heart and face,—
Not to betray the doomed and splendid race
You are so proud of, to which you belong.
For trouble comes to all of us: the rat
Has courage, in adversity, to fight;
But what a shining animal is man,
Who knows, when pain subsides, that is not that,
For worse than that must follow—yet can write
Music; can laugh; play tennis; even plan.

I, being born a woman, and distressed
By all the needs and notions of my kind,
Am urged by your propinquity to find
Your person fair, and feel a certain zest
To bear your body's weight upon my breast:
So subtly is the fume of life designed,
To clarify the pulse and cloud the mind,
And leave me once again undone, possessed.
Think not for this, however, the poor treason
Of my stout blood against my staggering brain,
I shall remember you with love, or season
My scorn with pity,—let me make it plain:
I find this frenzy insufficient reason
For conversation when we meet again.

What lips my lips have kissed, and where, and why,
I have forgotten, and what arms have lain
Under my head till morning; but the rain
Is full of ghosts tonight, that tap and sigh
Upon the glass and listen for reply,
And in my heart there stirs a quiet pain
For unremembered lads that not again
Will turn to me at midnight with a cry.
Thus in the winter stands the lonely tree,

Nor knows what birds have vanished one by one,
Yet knows its boughs more silent than before:
I cannot say what loves have come and gone,
I only know that summer sang in me
A little while, that in me sings no more.

(Move to chair)

Eugen: It's wonderful to write to you, my dearest. It takes the sting out of almost everything I find. I wanted you so last night. I was pretty unhappy—and, of course, tired too. Well, darling, I've poured out all my troubles. None of them matters when I think of you.

It's amusing to think how entirely, totally, absolutely different everything would be if you were here beside me. It makes me laugh, it's so funny that there could be such a difference.

Oh, it will be so lovely when we go around the earth together! I told some people yesterday that we are going to Java and China in March. Why not? For we are. We are. Aren't we?

(Stand and move to back of chair)

July 1924, Hong Kong Harbor. Dearest Mother: All day almost the spray of the ship was full of bright rainbows, and last night the phosphorous made the edge of the waves all like green electric light, and there was heat lightning, and I said, "Oh, Eugen, rainbows by day and phosphorous by night. I can hardly bear it." And he said, "If you should see a rainbow at night I don't think you could bear it." And just at the moment he finished speaking there was a flash of lightning, and across the phosphorescent crest of the wave, a beautiful perfect rainbow appeared, bright for a moment and instantly was gone. And I did bear it! I think not many people have seen a rainbow made by lightning or phosphorous. I am having the most thrilling time.—So much love from both of us.

(Move center stage)

When they came back they bought a home high in the Berkshire Hills. Eugen took the overgrown and neglected land and turned it into a fine prosperous farm. They named it Steepletop after a tall, pink wildflower that grew there.

(Go up platform steps and sit on bench)

June 1925, Steepletop. Dearest Mother: Here we are in one of the loveliest places in the world, I'm sure, working like Trojans, dogs, slaves, etc., having chimneys put in and plumbing put in and a garage built. And we found a brook—an extra one that we didn't know was there. All it needs is a fourth wall to make a swimming pool. The expenses are staggering. The furnace and bathroom alone cost over a thousand dollars. But it's going to be a sweet place when it's finished, and it's ours, all ours. Seven hundred acres of land and a lovely house and no rent to pay.

> I know not how such things can be;
> I only know there came to me
> A fragrance such as never clings
> To aught save happy living things;
> A sound as of some joyous elf
> Singing sweet songs to please himself,
> And, through and over everything
> A sense of glad awakening.

Dearest Darlings: We decided to postpone the installation of our individual baths until the dormer windows are in, and the installation of the dormer windows until the terrace is laid, and the laying of the terrace until the swimming pool is dug, and the digging of the swimming pool until we can get enough money to buy some cocoa butter against sunburn.—We have very little gin left. It takes just about all we can get from day to day to keep the men laying brick. The only trouble with our plumbing is that we have no water. So we all took a bath in the brook. I made the boys give me upstream because I was cleaner.—OH! We found rhubarb and asparagus entirely hidden under a forest of tansy. And while we were hunting wild strawberries we came upon a whole plot of tame one. (That's what Eugen calls the others.) We have a large apple orchard too.

> And all at once the heavy night
> Fell from my eyes, and I could see!—
> A drenched and dripping apple tree;
> A last long line of silver rain,
> A sky grown clear and blue again.
> And as I looked a quickening gust
> Of wind blew up to me and thrust
> Into my face a miracle
> Of orchard-breath, and with the smell,—
> I know not how such things can be!—
> I breathed my soul back into me.

To Frank Crownenshield, Editor of Vanity Fair:

Dear Crownie: What a nice person you are! Eugen thinks so too. I have started work at last on the book of the opera to which Deems Taylor is writing the music. It's to be called "The King's Henchmen." It will be done the beginning of summer. And then, a year late, the articles for Vanity Fair will begin to come in. You've been a darling, Crownie, as I believe I said before. Give my love to Elinore Wylie.

Elinore Wylie was one of her contemporaries whom she dearly loved. Vincent had written poems about her. One of them describes her this way:

> Oh, she was beautiful in every part!—
> The auburn hair that bound the subtle brain,
> The lovely mouth cut clear by wit and pain,
> Uttering oaths and nonsense, uttering art
> In casual speech.

She passionately admired her as a poet, and was deeply devoted to her as a friend. So when an organization of women writers had discriminated against Elinore Wylie because of some aspect of her personal life, Vincent's indignation blazed.

(*Take center stage*)

April, 1927. Ladies: I have received from you recently several communications inviting me to be your guest of honor at a function to take place in Washington sometime this month. I replied not only that I was unable to attend but that I regretted this inability. I said that I was sensible to the honor you did me and that I hoped you would invite me again.

Your recent gross and shocking insolence to one of the most distinguished writers of our time has changed all that.

It is not in the power of an organization which has insulted Elinore Wylie to honor me! And indeed I should feel it unbecoming on my part to sit as guest of honor in a gathering of writers where honor is tendered, not so much for one's literary accomplishment as for the circumspection of one's personal life. Believe me, if the eminent object of your pusillanimous attack has not directed her movements in conformity with your timid philosophies, no more have I mine. I, too, am eligible for your disesteem. Strike me too from your lists, and permit me, I beg you, to share with Elinore Wylie a brilliant exile from your fusty province.—Yours very truly, Edna St. Vincent Millay.

ACT III

"The soul can split the sky in two
And let the face of God shine through"

(*Lights full up. Enter from Stage Right*)

**Before she has her floor swept
Or her dishes done,
Any day you'll find her
A-sunning in the sun!**

**It's long after midnight
Her key's in the lock,
And you never see her chimney smoke
Till past ten o'clock!**

**She digs in her garden
With a shovel and a spoon,
She weeds her lazy lettuce
By the light of the moon,**

**She walks up the walk
Like a woman in a dream,
She forgets she borrowed butter
And pays you back in cream!**

**Her lawn looks like a meadow,
And if she mows the place**

She leaves the clover standing
And the Queen Ann's Lace!

(*Sit at desk*)

Steepletop, 1928. Dearest Mother: And I have been working on a new book of poems that is finished at last. I put up some plums today and some tomatoes too, off our own place. They look so pretty on the table in rows with the sun shining through them. Eugen is driving down the hill for the mail now, so I must hurry this into an envelope. So much love from us both.— P.S. I have baked beans in the oven—and on Friday! Do you suppose they will refuse to bake at all? I'm sure they're as indignant as anything.

(*While crossing to chair*)

As I sat down by Saddle Stream
To bathe my dusty feet there,
A boy was standing on the bridge
Any girl would meet there.

As I went over Woody Knob
And dipped into the hollow,
A youth was coming up the hill
Any maid would follow.

Then in I turned at my own gate,—
And nothing to be sad for—
To such a man as any wife
Would pass a pretty lad for.

(*Sit in chair*)

February 1929. We have been snowed in—I mean hermetically—four weeks today. Five miles on snowshoes, that means, to fetch the mail or to post a letter. And the thermometer at zero again this morning. We can get out—but we're never quite sure of getting back up the hill. All the old beams and boards that were no good for anything else, have been sawn up and stacked in the most beautiful woodpile you ever saw.

> Pile high the hickory and the light
> Log of chestnut struck by the blight.
> Welcome-in the winter night.
>
> The day has gone in hewing and felling,
> Sawing and drawing wood to the dwelling
> For the night of talk and story-telling.
>
> These are the hours that give the edge
> To the blunted axe and the bent wedge,
> Straighten the saw and lighten the sledge.
>
> Here are question and reply,
> And the fire reflected in the thinking eye.
> So peace, and let the bob-cat cry.

Dear Kids: This is to invite you to a grand house party to be thrown at Steepletop, June 21st to 24th, or as long as everything—meaning hosts, guests and liquor holds out. There will be about fifty souls—poets and musicians included. Please tell us at once that you will come.

August 1930. Dearest Mother, It is three years since I walked up and down in front of the State House in Boston and carried a placard protesting the execution of Sacco and Vanzetti and was arrested and taken to jail for this. Last night I spoke in Boston on the third anniversary of the execution—and read some of

my poems. But I'll tell you all about that later. Lots
and lots of love.

September 1930. Mother dear: I hope the reason
why you haven't written for so long is that you are
busy and having a good time—not that you are not
feeling well or something. We will be down to see you
very soon. Please let us hear from you, darling, as
soon as you feel like writing. We are a little worried
about you. Eugen sends his love too.

April 1931. Darlings: I knew that you were sorry
about Mother but there's nothing to say. We had a
grand time, but it's a changed world. The presence
of that absence is everywhere.

> The courage that my mother had
> Went with her, and is with her still:
> Rock from New England quarried;
> Now granite in a granite hill.
>
> The golden brooch my mother wore
> She left behind for me to wear;
> I have no thing I treasure more:
> Yet, it is something I could spare.
>
> Oh, if instead she'd left to me
> The thing she took into the grave!—
> That courage like a rock, which she
> Has no more need of, and I have.

Her mother was dead and the previous year her
friend Elinore Wylie had died.

> I am not resigned to the shutting away of loving
>   hearts in the hard ground.
> So it is, and so it will be, for so it has been, time

out of mind:
Into the darkness they go, the wise and the lovely. Crowned
With lillies and with laurel they go; but I am not resigned.
Down, down, down into the darkness of the grave
Gently they go, the beautiful, the tender, the kind;
Quietly they go, the intelligent, the witty, the brave.
I know. But I do not approve. And I am not resigned.

November 1935. Dear Editors: The author is fully aware that she has advised the publishers at least twice as to her preference concerning the number of stanzas to a page. She is further aware that the publishers have paid not the slightest attention to said preference on the part of the author. The author respectfully submits that not even those lovely bits of colored paper which the publishers sent her to play with have quite succeeded in taking her mind off the main issue. I am enclosing A—the samples of end paper and dust cover; B—a few more changes to be incorporated in my manuscript, and C—two asperins.

Yours for a carefree winter,

Edna St. Vincent Millay

December 1940. ... The reason you have not heard from me in so long is that for the past four years—in fact, ever since 1936—I have been sick, or rather, not sick, simply in constant pain due to an injury to certain nerves in my back, referred to by ten or twelve different doctors as nerves four, five and six of the dorsal spine—referred to by me as that place under my right shoulderblade. The nerve injury is a result of my having been thrown out of the station wagon one night—not by the driver, as you are probably thinking, but by the sudden swinging open of a door against which I was leaning. I've had three operations and would be quite well now, I think, except that I am still, naturally, rather weak.

Eugen says he is not pleased with God. Anyway, never mind all that. It is not important. It does not matter because I have been able to work. I am sending you my new book "Make Bright the Arrows." It is subtitled "1940 Notebook," and that's what it really is. A piece of impassioned war-time propaganda—not poems, posters—acres of bad poetry into which a few good poems got bound up because they happened to be propaganda too. I can tell you from my own experience that there is nothing on this earth which can so get on the nerves of a good poet as writing bad poetry. I know bad poetry as well as the next one. But perhaps you'll forgive it, and me for what I'm trying to do.

Merry Christmas and all my love,

Edna.

To Harper and Bros.—1941. Once again I must ask my publishers to come—come running to my aid. What it comes to is this. Because of the war Eugen has lost everything he had. There's not a penny he can get at, so for the time being it's up to me.

Now, however, I think the answer to the pain may have been hit on. I shall probably get well soon and be able to get back to work. (I really have been working very hard a great part of the time.) I've tried to do a little typing but have had to give it up after half a page or so. Eating with a knife and fork is something close to excruciating. Seldom has morphine seemed so slow in getting to me, although poor Eugen, who hates like hell to have to give it to me, he's quicker with it than the doctor by now. Can Harper's help me as per enclosed list of my needs?—Affectionately, Edna.

—Eugen has been desperate about me. Day and night he has nursed me. He has written no word to anyone. His face has been gray with anxiety. But now I am beginning to have moments, even hours, when I am not in pain. He will be more like himself soon. Do you remember how you told me to go to sleep on a plank? I slept on a plank for five months.

—Eugen would send his love but he's just gone down to milk the cows.

1943—The young wrens who have their house under the peak of the ice house are flying this morning, and what a to-do, and what beautiful singing from their father; as if to say, "Someday you'll have as handsome feathers as I, and a tail that sticks straight up behind your rump, and a song as beautiful as mine. You boys, that is, and even you girls will have fun engineering long twigs through small doorways."

1946—and I have also learned by heart of Shelley not only "To the West Wind" but also "Hymn to Intellectual Beauty," a devil to learn by heart. Anyway, I have them all now. And what evil thing can ever again brush me with its wings? I am really cured of the pain under my shoulder. You are glad.

(Rise and go behind chair)

I remember the nasturtiums, the climbing ones that grew every summer over the porch of our house in Camden, Maine. I wish I could see a gooseberry bush again, and a very small orchard of quince trees—and a Russet apple tree. If I ever see a Russet apple tree again I shall climb it, and with a book in my hand. And I shall sit in that tree for hours hidden by the leaves, reading "Hero and Leander," of "As You Like

It." Why, this morning I do not know at all whether the rain has really stopped and the sun is actually shining, or whether it is just my childhood that I see.

(Sit on arm of chair)

> As sharp as in my childhood, still
> Ecstasy shocks me fixed. The will
> Cannot entice it, never could,
> So never tries. But from the wood
> The wind will hurl the clashing sleet;
> Or a small fawn with lovely feet,
> Uncertain in its gait, will walk
> Among the ferns, not breaking back
> One frond, not bruising one fern black,
> Into the clearing, and appraise
> With mild, attracted, wondering gaze,
> And lifted head unhurt and new,
> The world that he was born into.
>
> Such marvels as, one time, I feared
> Might go, and leave me unprepared
> For hardship. But they never did.
> They blaze before me still as wild
> And clear, as when I was a child.
> They never went away at all.
> I need not, though I do, recall
> Such moments in my childhood, when
> Wonder sprang out at me again,
> And took me by the heels, and whirled
> Me round and round above the world.
>
> For wonder leaps upon me still,
> And makes me dizzy, makes me ill,
> But never frightened—for I know—
> Not where—but in whose hands I go:
> The lovely fingers of Delight
> Have hold of me and hold me tight.

ACT III   A LOVELY LIGHT

(Center stage)

Vincent had always loved the sea. It was what she missed the most from her childhood. So they bought a small island off the coast of Maine. It was called Ragged Island. It had its own harbor and their cottage was the only dwelling place on it. Steepletop, of course, remained their home, but now they also had an island of their own and Vincent had back the climate of the sea—the climate of her childhood.

This is not a letter that was written and posted to someone far away. It is just a note that she had scribbled in pencil and left in the cottage for Eugen to find.

It was written in September of 1947.

(Seated in chair)

Darling Eugen: You have just gone down to the harbor again. It seems only a moment since we both came up from the harbor. You drenched to the skin; I shining and excited almost to—that's the French word for it?—not translution—certainly not transport—what the hell is it?—Anyway, watching it at a safe distance until you called me to help you with the ropes. And what a silly knife you have. It doesn't cut at all—a sharp-edged stone would have done better. I could have done better with my teeth. But things you do with your teeth do things to your teeth in return.

Darling, come up from the harbor. The sea is making, at least it looks so, and anyway the wind is coming up northwest by north, I think. Don't go out please. There's no need to tackle it. We have everything here. Dearest, I'm going top side. Maybe I'll sleep—maybe not.

(While crossing to stand at desk)

The hills may shift, the waters may decline,
Winter may twist the stem from the twig that bore it
But never your love from me, your hand from mine.

December 1947. Dearest Crowney: We spent the summer on our own island. Ragged Island in Casco Bay. It looked for a time as if we would have to spend the winter there as well. We'd stayed on much later than usual, and got caught in the autumn storms. Luckily, we had plenty of provisions, and the surf, of course, was magnificent, so we had great fun. But we didn't get back to Steepletop until damn near time to slide the Thanksgiving turkey into the oven. (*Take shawl from chair back, where it has been placed, wrap it around you while walking*)

Ah, broken garden, frost on the melons and on the beans!
Frozen are the ripe tomatoes, the red fruit and the hairy golden stem;
Frozen are the grapes, and the vine above them frozen, and the peppers are frozen!
And I walk among them smiling,—for what of them?

I will cook for my love a banquet of beets and cabbages,
Leeks, potatoes, turnips, all such fruits...
For my clever love, who has returned from further than the far east;
We will laugh like spring above the steaming, stolid winter roots.

ACT III A LOVELY LIGHT 45

(*Sitting at desk*)

1949. Dear Friend: You feared that I might be ill. I am far worse than ill. My husband has died. I can not write about it nor about anything else and I can not answer questions. But I wanted to get some word to you, you were so distressed by my silence. The books came early in November. I have not yet been able to read them, but I thank you very much.—Good luck to you. Sincerely, Edna St. Vincent Millay.

(*Center stage, then back to desk*)

Eugen Boissevain had died in August of 1949. When suddenly he learned the seriousness of his condition —having suffered no apparent illness—he told no one. He just quietly put their affairs in order and then went to the hospital. Vincent was with him during the terrible days and nights, trying to take over his pain, trying to help him to breathe. The last words he spoke were: "It was good while it lasted."

Then when it was over—when everything was over, she returned to Steepletop to live alone. Her friends protested but she went anyway. A hired man came in the mornings to do the outside chores, and two days a week a woman from a neighboring farm came in to clean or to wash and iron. She was alone at Steepletop. That was what she wanted.

She wrote to her friend who ran the post office in the village five miles away:

Dear Mary: Thank you for all your kindness. I don't know how I should have managed without your help. Yes, it must indeed seem impossible to you that he will not be coming down the hill to fetch the mail this lovely autumn day. He never comes up the hill either, anymore.

(*Walking*)

As to some lovely temple, tenantless
Long since, that once was sweet with shivering
   brass,
Knowing well its altars ruined and the grass
Grown up between the stones, yet from excess
Of grief hard driven, or great loneliness,
The worshiper returns, and those who pass
Marvel his crying on a name that was,—
So is it now with me in my distress.
Your body was a temple to Delight;
Cold are its ashes whence the breath is fled;
Yet here one time your spirit was wont to move;
Here might I hope to find you day or night;
And here I come to look for you, my love,
Even now, foolishly, knowing you are dead.

(Sitting at desk)

December 1949. To her friends in New York:
Dear Margaret and Alive: If you chaps are determined to give me a Christmas present nothing I can say will stop you—not that I want to stop you—and now I will tell you what I would like for Christmas.

A—Three typewriter ribbons

B—Six composition books, the kind with stiff covers so that I can pick one up and prop it against my knee and scribble in it. Query—does A plus B indicate creative cerebration? In a way, yes. If there's anything more stimulating to such activity than a brand new typewriter ribbon, it's a brand new composition book with stiff covers. Oh, I should feel so rich, so reinforced, so sassy with a new ribbon in each of my three typewriters.

All the pine cones are deep under now.

                                   Love—Quickly,

To Mr. Cass Canfield—Harper and Bros.

Dear Cass: I meant to write you at once after sending you that telegram last November, for I realized the moment it had gone how abrupt and chilly it might sound. Cass—the reason I wired you not to come was because it suddenly occured to me that that would be the day after Thanksgiving, and I was not at all sure how I would get through the first Thanksgiving Day I had ever spent all alone. I got through it all right, and all the other happy holidays too, by simply by-passing them. (I love that expression.) On Christmas Eve the only thing I did by way of observance was to sit at the piano and play and sing some Christmas carols. And on New Year's Eve I telephoned Eugen's family in Holland. I knew they would talk of Eugen and that they would be worrying about me. For they love me as I do them.

April 1950. Dear Mary: You wonder how I am going to stand the spring. I'm wondering myself I can tell you. And I'm plenty scared. Not scared that I shan't muddle through in some way or other—just scared. Scared the way I used to be as a child when I had to go to the dentist, in the days before they gave you novacaine. I have already encountered the first dandelion. I stood and stared at it with a kind of horror. And then suddenly I felt ashamed of myself and sorry for the dandelion. How excited he always was when he saw the first dandelion. And long before the plants were big enough for even a rabbit to find them, he had dug a fine mess, for greens. He used to say "pick dandelions" and I would say, "Not pick, Dig." And he would say, "Don't scold poor Eugen. He does so his best." Alas, alas and alas.

Ragged Island is not for sale. As soon as I can bear it I shall go back there. I am working terribly hard. The Thanksgiving number of The Saturday Evening

Post will have a new poem of mine which I hope you will read. Oh, I know I'm making a big fuss about a small piece of work—but it's so wonderful to be writing again.—My only hope just now. This is a bad time of year for me.

(Center stage)

    She was writing again. She was working on a sonnet. It is written, with corrections, with words crossed out and alternative words written in—and at the bottom of the page three lines are circled in pencil.
    On some brilliant October morning she must have stepped through her doorway unprepared when Wonder sprang out at her again. For these are the words that were found in the composition book with stiff covers.—

> Never before, perhaps was such a sight!
> Only one sky, my breath, and all that blue!
> Creation blue—worlds morning
> And room too for clouds
> Long sprays of Egret thin and bright
> And dumpling clouds, horizon bound, thick white.
>
> I will control myself or go inside.
> I will not flaw perfection with my grief.
> Handsome this day no matter who has died.

(All lights dimmed except for 'dawn' light)

Dear Lena: The iron is set too high. Don't put it on where it says "Linen" or it will scorch the linen.

Try it on "Rayon" and then perhaps on "Woolen".—
And Lena, be careful not to burn your fingers when you shift it from one heat to another.

It is five-thirty and I have been working all night. I'm going to bed.

GOOD MORNING

(Walk up steps to platform and exit stage left)

Other Publications for Your Interest

TALKING WITH...
(LITTLE THEATRE)
By JANE MARTIN

11 women—Bare stage

Here, at last, is the collection of eleven extraordinary monologues for eleven actresses which had them on their feet cheering at the famed Actors Theatre of Louisville—audiences, critics and, yes, even jaded theatre professionals. The mysteriously pseudonymous Jane Martin is truly a "find", a new writer with a wonderfully idiosyncratic style, whose characters alternately amuse, move and frighten us always, however, speaking to use from the depths of their souls. The characters include a baton twirler who has found God through twirling; a fundamentalist snake handler, an ex-rodeo rider crowded out of the life she has cherished by men in 3-piece suits who want her to dress up "like Minnie damn Mouse in a tutu"; an actress willing to go to any length to get a job; and an old woman who claims she once saw a man with "cerebral walrus" walk into a McDonald's and be healed by a Big Mac. "Eleven female monologues, of which half a dozen verge on brilliance."—London Guardian. "Whoever (Jane Martin) is, she's a writer with an original imagination."—Village Voice. "With Jane Martin, the monologue has taken on a new poetic form, intensive in its method and revelatory in its impact."—Philadelphia Inquirer. "A dramatist with an original voice . . . (these are) tales about enthusiasms that become obsessions, eccentric confessionals that levitate with religious symbolism and gladsome humor."—N.Y. Times. *Talking With . . .* is the 1982 winner of the American Theatre Critics Association Award for Best Regional Play. (#22009)

(Royalty, $60-$40.
If individual monologues are done separately: Royalty, $15-$10.)

HAROLD AND MAUDE
(ADVANCED GROUPS—COMEDY)
By COLIN HIGGINS

9 men, 8 women—Various settings

Yes: *the Harold and Maude!* This is a stage adaptation of the wonderful movie about the suicidal 19 year-old boy who finally learns how to truly *live* when he meets up with that delightfully whacky octogenarian, Maude. Harold is the proverbial Poor Little Rich Kid. His alienation has caused him to attempt suicide several times, though these attempts are more cries for attention than actual attempts. His peculiar attachment to Maude, whom he meets at a funeral (a mutual passion), is what saves him—and what captivates us. This new stage version, a hit in France directed by the internationally-renowned Jean-Louis Barrault, will certainly delight both afficionados of the film and new-comers to the story. "Offbeat upbeat comedy."—Christian Science Monitor. (#10032)

(Royalty, $60-$40.)

HOME-BUILT
Lighting Equipment
for The Small Stage
By THEODORE FUCHS

This volume presents a series of fourteen simplified designs for building various types of stage lighting and control equipment, with but one purpose in mind—to enable the amateur producer to acquire a complete set of stage lighting equipment at the lowest possible cost. The volume is 8½" x 11" in size, with heavy paper and spiral binding—features which make the volume well suited to practical workshop use.

Community Theatre
A MANUAL FOR SUCCESS
By JOHN WRAY YOUNG

The ideal text for anyone interested in participating in Community Theatre as a vocation or avocation. "Organizing a Community Theatre," "A Flight Plan for the Early Years," "Programming for People—Not Computers," and other chapters are blueprints for solid growth. "Technical, Business and Legal Procedures" cuts a safe and solvent path through some tricky undergrowth. Essential to the library of all community theatres, and to the schools who will supply them with talent in the years to come.

FAVORITE BROADWAY DRAMAS
from
SAMUEL FRENCH, INC.

ALL THE WAY HOME – THE AMEN CORNER – AMERICAN BUFFALO – ANASTASIA – ANGEL STREET – BECKET – THE BELLE OF AMHERST – BUTLEY – COLD STORAGE – COME BACK, LITTLE SHEBA – A DAY IN THE DEATH OF JOE EGG – A DELICATE BALANCE – THE DESPERATE HOURS – THE ELEPHANT MAN – EQUUS – FORTUNE AND MEN'S EYES – A HATFUL OF RAIN – THE HOMECOMING – J.B. – KENNEDY'S CHILDREN – LOOK HOMEWARD, ANGEL – A MAN FOR ALL SEASONS – THE MIRACLE WORKER – A MOON FOR THE MISBEGOTTEN – NO PLACE TO BE SOMEBODY – ONE FLEW OVER THE CUCKOO'S NEXT – OUR TOWN – A RAISIN IN THE SUN – THE RIVER NIGER – THE SHADOW BOX – SIX CHARACTERS IN SEARCH OF AN AUTHOR – STICKS AND BONES – THE SUBJECT WAS ROSES – TEA AND SYMPATHY – THE VISIT – WINGS

For descriptions of all our plays, consult our Basic Catalogue of Plays

A Breeze from The Gulf

MART CROWLEY

(Little Theatre) Drama

The author of "The Boys in the Band" takes us on a journey back to a small Mississippi town to watch a 15-year-old boy suffer through adolescence to adulthood and success as a writer. His mother is a frilly southern doll who has nothing to fall back on when her beauty fades. She develops headaches and other physical problems, while the asthmatic son turns to dolls and toys at an age when other boys are turning to sports. The traveling father becomes withdrawn, takes to drink; and mother takes to drugs to kill the pain of the remembrances of, things past. She eventually ends in an asylum, and the father in his fumbling way tries to tell the son to live the life he must.

> "The boy is plunged into a world of suffering he didn't create. . . . One of the most electrifying plays I've seen in the past few years . . . Scenes boil and hiss . . . The dialogue goes straight to the heart." Reed, Sunday News.

Royalty, $50–$35

ECHOES

N. RICHARD NASH

(All Groups) Drama
2 Men, 1 Woman, Interior

A young man and woman build a low-keyed paradise of happiness within an asylum, only to have it shattered by the intrusion of the outside world. The two characters search, at times agonizingly to determine the difference between illusion and reality. The effort is lightened at times by moments of shared love and "pretend" games, like decorating Christmas trees that are not really there. The theme of love, vulnerable to the surveillances of the asylum, and the ministrations of the psychiatrist, (a non-speaking part) seems as fragile in the constrained setting as it often is in the outside world.

> ". . . even with the tragic, sombre theme there is a note of hope and possible release and the situations presented specifically also have universal applications to give it strong effect . . . intellectual, but charged with emotion."—Reed.

Royalty, $50–$35

HANDBOOK
for
THEATRICAL APPRENTICES
By Dorothy Lee Tompkins

Here is a common sense book on theatre, fittingly subtitled, "A Practical Guide in All Phases of Theatre." Miss Tompkins has wisely left art to the artists and written a book which deals only with the practical side of the theatre. All the jobs of the theatre are categorized, from the star to the person who sells soft drinks at intermission. Each job is defined, and its basic responsibilities given in detail. An invaluable manual for every theatre group in explaining to novices the duties of apprenticeship, and in reassessing its own organizational structure and functions.

"If you are an apprentice or are just aspiring in any capacity, then you'll want to read and own Dorothy Lee Tompkins' A HANDBOOK FOR THEATRICAL APPRENTICES. It should be required reading for any drama student anywhere and is a natural for the amateur in any phase of the theatre."—George Freedley, Morning Telegraph.

"It would be helpful if the HANDBOOK FOR THEATRICAL APPRENTICES were in school or theatrical library to be used during each production as a guide to all participants."—Florence E. Hill, Dramatics Magazine.

Bible Herstory

PATRICIA MONTLEY

(May Double.) Satire.

18 females—Bare Stage

Bible Herstory, a one-act feminist satire in six scenes featuring an all-woman cast. In "Paradise Abandoned," Eve convinces God not to stifle Her creativity just because She made a mistake in creating Adam. In "Noah's Ark-itect," Noah's wife and daughter prepare for the flood and "inspire" Noah to build a boat. "The Sacrifice of Sarah" shows Abraham's wife working on a theatrical project to save a lazy Isaac's life. In "Miriam in Labor," Moses' sister bargains with Pharaoh's daughter for better working conditions. In "Queen Solomon and the Paternity Suit," her Majesty proposes to cut in half a philandering charioteer claimed by both wife and mistress. In "The Renunciation," Mary rejects the Angel Gabriella's offer of the saviorship of the world, but agrees to have a son. $2.00.

(Royalty, $20-$15.)

Out of Our Father's House

Play with music. (All Groups.)

BASED ON EVE MERRIAM'S
Growing Up Female in America: Ten Lives

3 females play 6 roles
Musicians—1 Interior

Arranged for the stage by Paula Wagner, Jack Hofsiss and Eve Merriam. Music by Ruth Cawford Seeger adapted by Daniel Schrier. With additional music by Daniel Shrier and Marjorie Lipari.

Taken entirely from diaries, journals and letters of the characters portrayed. They are a schoolgirl—founder of the Women's Suffrage Movement, an astronomer, a labor organizer, a minister, a doctor and a woman coming out of the Jewish ghetto. They are watched as they grow up, marry and bear children. They do not covet men's jobs, but when they want careers they are ostracized. A very moving play seen through the words and eyes of 19th century American women. $1.00. Write for information about music.

(Royalty, $20-$15.)

Other Publications for Your Interest

AGNES OF GOD
(LITTLE THEATRE—DRAMA)

By JOHN PIELMEIER

3 women—1 set (bare stage)

Doctor Martha Livingstone, a court-appointed psychiatrist, is asked to determine the sanity of a young nun accused of murdering her own baby. Mother Miriam Ruth, the nun's superior, seems bent on protecting Sister Agnes from the doctor, and Livingstone's suspicions are immediately aroused. In searching for solutions to various mysteries (who killed the baby? Who fathered the child?) Livingstone forces all three women, herself included, to face some harsh realities in their own lives, and to re-examine the meaning of faith and the commitment of love. "Riveting, powerful, electrifying new drama . . . three of the most magnificent performances you will see this year on any stage anywhere . . . the dialogue crackles."—Rex Reed, N.Y. Daily News. ". . . outstanding play . . . deals intelligently with questions of religion and psychology."—Mel Gussow, N.Y. Times. ". . . unquestionably blindingly theatrical . . . cleverly executed blood and guts evening in the theatre . . . three sensationally powered performances calculated to wring your withers."—Clive Barnes, N.Y. Post. (#236)

(For Future Release.
Royalty, $60-$40, when available.)
(Posters available)

COME BACK TO THE 5 & DIME, JIMMY DEAN, JIMMY DEAN
(ADVANCED GROUPS—DRAMA)

By ED GRACZYK

1 man, 8 women—Interior

In a small-town dime store in West Texas, the Disciples of James Dean gather for their twentieth reunion. Now a gaggle of middle-aged women, the Disciples were teenagers when Dean filmed "Giant" two decades ago in nearby Marfa. One of them, an extra in the film, has a child whom she says was conceived by Dean on the "Giant" set; the child is the Jimmy Dean of the title. The ladies' reminiscences mingle with flash-backs to their youth; then the arrival of a stunning and momentarily unrecognized woman sets off a series of confrontations that upset their self-deceptions and expose their well-hidden disappointments. "Full of homespun humor . . . surefire comic gems."—N.Y. Post. "Captures convincingly the atmosphere of the 1950s."—Women's Wear Daily. (#5147)

(Royalty, $60-$40.)